now you're cookin'
THAI

Colophon

© 2003 Rebo International b.v., Lisse, The Netherlands

This 4th edition reprinted in 2006.

Original recipes and photographs: © R&R Publishing Pty. Ltd.

Design, editing, production, and layout: Minkowsky Graphics, Enkhuizen, The Netherlands

Cover design: Minkowsky Graphics, Enkhuizen, The Netherlands

Translation and adaptation: American Pie, London and Sunnyvale, California

ISBN 13: 978-90-366-1958-5

ISBN 10: 90-366-1958-0

now you're cookin'
THAI

THIS BOOK JUST MAKES YOU WANNA COOK

REBO
PUBLISHERS

Foreword

Welcome to Thai cuisine. In Thailand, the art of cooking is practiced in a way that combines the influences of neighboring countries with national dishes, to which the varying and contrasting tastes are witness.

Throughout the centuries, Thai cuisine has developed a unique style that excels in creativity. Try out all recipes but only take small bites. The Thais think it is bad-mannered to eat large portions, they consider it may indicate that they have not been generous enough in serving you. In Thailand, people love to snack. The Thais believe you should eat whenever you are hungry. So dig in!

Abbreviations

tbsp = tablespoon

tsp = teaspoon

g = gram

kg = kilogram

fl oz = fluid ounce

lb = pound

oz = ounce

ml = milliliter

l = liter

°C = degree Celsius

°F = degree Fahrenheit

Where three measurements are given, the

first is the American cup measure.

Method

Cut the chicken into ½in/1cm strips. Brush the chicken strips with 1 tbsp/15ml peanut oil and broil or pan-fry until the chicken is golden-brown and slightly charred, about 3 minutes each side.

Heat the remaining 1 tbsp/15ml peanut oil in a large saucepan and add the garlic, shallots, chopped coriander leaves and stems, ginger, chopped chili peppers, sliced lemongrass, and finely shredded lime leaves, and toss in the hot oil until fragrant, about two minutes. Add the broth and bring to the boil. Simmer for 10 minutes then add the broiled chicken strips and simmer for a further 10 minutes.

Add the Thai fish sauce and Chinese rice noodles and simmer for a further two minutes, or until the noodles are tender.

Add the sliced green onions (scallions), lime juice, and coriander leaves and serve very hot.

* Available from oriental food stores.

Ingredients

3 x 7oz/200g chicken breast fillets

2 tbsp/30ml peanut oil

4 cloves garlic, minced

2 shallots, chopped

5 stems of coriander, leaves included

30g/1oz piece ginger, bruised

3 small red chili peppers, chopped

Hot-and-Sour Chicken **Soup**

3 stalks lemongrass, finely sliced

6 kaffir lime leaves, finely shredded*

8 cups/3½ pints/2 l chicken or vegetable broth

3 tbsp/45ml Thai fish sauce*

⅓ cup/31/2 oz/100g dry cellophane or glass noodles*

6 green onions (scallions), diagonally sliced

1–2 limes, juice squeezed

handful of coriander (cilantro) leaves

Thai

Method

To cook the rice, bring a large pot of salted water to the boil. Add the rice and simmer for 8-10 minutes or until tender. Drain and rinse thoroughly in cold water then drain again.

Meanwhile, make the dressing. Whisk together the oil, lime juice, fish sauce, palm sugar, sweet chili sauce, ginger, chili powder and salt and pepper. Reserve until the rice is ready.

Prepare all the vegetables then mix thoroughly with the finely sliced lime leaves, coriander, chopped roasted peanuts, and sesame seeds. Add the cooked rice and mix well.

Toss the rice and vegetable mixture thoroughly with the dressing, then add the Thai basil and serve.

Gingered **Thai Rice Salad**

Ingredients

2 cups/1 lb/500g long-grain rice

5 green onions (scallions), finely chopped on the diagonal

3 medium carrots, coarsely grated

4 baby bok choy, washed and chopped

2 kaffir lime leaves

½ cup/2oz/50g coarsely chopped coriander

1½ cups/12oz/350g chopped roasted peanuts

1 tbsp/15g black sesame seeds

2 tbsp/30g finely chopped Thai basil

Dressing:

2 tbsp/30ml vegetable or peanut oil

juice of 2 limes (about 3 tbsp)

3 tbsp/45ml Thai fish sauce

2 tbsp/60g palm sugar

2 tbsp/30ml sweet chili sauce

1 tbsp/15g minced ginger

pinch of chili powder or cayenne pepper

salt and pepper to taste

Thai

Method

1. Place shallots, chili peppers, lime leaves, ginger, and broth in a saucepan and bring to the boil over a high heat. Reduce heat and simmer for 3 minutes.

2. Add fish, shrimp, mussels, and mushrooms and cook for 3-5 minutes or until fish and seafood are cooked. Discard any mussels that do not open after 5 minutes cooking. Stir in lime juice and fish sauce. To serve, ladle soup into bowls, scatter with coriander (cilantro) leaves and accompany with lime wedges.

Note:

Straw mushrooms are one of the most popular mushrooms used in Asian cooking and are easy to find in cans. Oyster mushrooms are also known as abalone mushrooms and range in color from white to gray to pale pink. Their shape is similar to that of an oyster shell and they have a delicate flavor. Oyster mushrooms should not be eaten raw as some people are allergic to them in the uncooked state.

Ingredients

4 red or golden shallots, sliced

2 fresh green chili peppers, chopped

6 kaffir lime leaves

4 slices fresh ginger

8 cups/3½ pints/2 l fish, chicken or vegetable broth

8oz/250g boneless firm fish fillets, cut into chunks

Hot-and-Sour **Seafood Soup**

12 medium raw shrimp, shelled and deveined

12 mussels, scrubbed and beards removed

1 cup/4oz/125g oyster or straw mushrooms

3 tbsp/45ml lime juice

2 tbsp/50ml Thai fish sauce (nam pla)

fresh coriander (cilantro) leaves

lime wedges

Thai

Method

1. Peel the outer covering from the lemongrass stalk, then finely chop the lower white bulbous part and discard the fibrous top.

2. Place the broth, fish sauce, sugar, lemongrass, chili pepper, garlic, and ginger in a saucepan. Bring to the boil, then reduce the heat and simmer, covered, for 10 minutes to release their flavors.

3. Add the chicken slices to the broth and cook for 2 minutes, then add the carrot, celery, and green onions (scallions) and cook for a further 5 minutes or until the vegetables and chicken are cooked and tender. Add the lime juice and herbs to the broth and heat through. Garnish with the shredded green onion.

Thai Broth with Chicken and Vegetables

Ingredients

1 stalk lemongrass

5 cups/2 pints/1.25l chicken broth

4 tbsp/60ml Thai fish sauce

1 tbsp/1oz/25g superfine (caster) sugar

1 red chili pepper, deseeded and sliced

1 clove garlic, sliced

1in/2½cm piece fresh root ginger, thinly sliced

3 skinless boneless chicken breasts, thinly sliced

1 carrot, cut into matchsticks

1 stick celery, sliced

5 green onions (scallions), 4 sliced, 1 shredded, to garnish

1 lime, juice squeezed

1 tbsp/15g each of roughly chopped fresh coriander (cilantro), mint, and basil

Method

1. Place noodles in a bowl and pour over boiling water to cover. Stand for 10 minutes, then drain well.

2. Heat oil in a frying pan over a high heat, add garlic and ginger and stir-fry for 1 minute. Add pork, stir-fry for 5 minutes or until pork is browned and cooked.

3. Arrange mint, coriander (cilantro), lettuce, shallots, chili pepper, and noodles on a serving platter. Top with pork mixture, then drizzle with lemon juice and soy sauce.

Ingredients

5oz/155g cellophane noodles

2 tsp/10ml sesame oil

2 cloves garlic, crushed

1 tbsp/15g finely grated fresh ginger

2 cups/1 lb/500g ground pork

½oz/15g mint leaves

½oz/15g coriander (cilantro) leaves

8 lettuce leaves

5 red or golden shallots, chopped

1 fresh red chili pepper, sliced

2 tbsp/30ml lemon juice

1 tbsp/15ml light soy sauce

Cellophane Noodle **Salad**

Note

Cellophane noodles also known as glass noodles and bean thread noodles or vermicelli are made from mung bean flour and are either very thin vermicelli-style noodles or flatter fettuccini-style noodles. In the dried state, they are very tough and difficult to break. For ease of use it is best to buy a brand which packages them as bundles.

Thai

Method

1. Heat oil in a wok over a medium heat. Add pork, water chestnuts, and lemongrass and stir-fry for 5 minutes or until pork is browned. Remove from wok and set aside to cool.

2. Place pork mixture, lime juice, and fish sauce in a bowl and mix to combine. Add beansprouts, green onions (scallions), mint, coriander (cilantro) and black pepper to taste, and toss gently.

3. Line a serving platter with lettuce leaves, then top with mangoes and pork mixture. Sprinkle with chopped hazelnuts or pecans.

Note:

This salad can be prepared to the end of step 2 several hours in advance. Cover and keep at room temperature. If preparing more than 2 hours in advance store in the refrigerator and remove 30 minutes before you are ready to assemble and serve it.

Minted Pork and Mango **Salad**

Ingredients

1 tbsp/15ml vegetable oil

2 cups/1 lb/500g lean ground pork

2 tbsp/2oz/60g canned water chestnuts, chopped

2 stalks fresh lemongrass, finely chopped

or 1 tsp dried lemongrass, soaked in hot water

until soft

2 tbsp/30ml lime juice

1 tbsp fish sauce

4 tbsp/2oz/60g bean sprouts

3 green onions (scallions), chopped

4 tbsp/60g chopped fresh mint

2 tbsp/30g chopped coriander (cilantro)

freshly ground black pepper

8oz/250g assorted lettuce leaves

2 mangoes, peeled and sliced

2oz/60g toasted hazelnuts or pecans, chopped

Thai

Method

Peel and chop the galangal and ginger. Remove the tough outer leaves of the lemongrass and chop the inner lemongrass finely. Finely chop the chili peppers and finely slice lime leaves and coriander stems and leaves.

In a large saucepan, heat the peanut oil and add the coriander seeds and chili peppers. Sauté for 2 minutes. Add the chopped galangal, ginger, lemongrass, lime leaves, and coriander stem and stir well over a high heat until the aromas become evident, about 5 minutes.

Turn down the heat and cover the pan with a lid. Cook for 30 minutes.

Meanwhile, make the shellfish broth. Place the fish and shellfish in a saucepan with the carrots, parsnip, onions, parsley, celery, and peppercorns and 10cups/5 pints/2½l of water. Bring to the boil then simmer for 1 hour, strain, and season to taste with salt and pepper.

To the aromatic vegetable mixture, add all the coconut milk and continue cooking for 30 minutes. Add the shellfish broth and simmer for 1 hour. Add the fish sauce, purée the soup thoroughly then strain, discarding any pulp. Season to taste with salt and pepper and serve garnished with very finely sliced Thai basil and mint leaves.

*When purchasing prawn and lobster shells and fish heads for broth, ask the fishmonger for whatever he has available. Generally, there will be plenty available that will be sold to you at an incredibly low price or perhaps it will even be given to you free of charge.

Ingredients

Soup

3 roots galangal

1 ginger root

5 stalks lemongrass

4 small red chili peppers

10 kaffir lime leaves

1 bunch coriander, stems included

1 tbsp/15ml peanut oil

2 tbsp/30g coriander seeds

3¾ cups/1½ pints/880ml cans Thai coconut milk

8 cups/2¾ pints/2 l shellfish broth

2 tbsp Thai fish sauce (nam pla)

Thai basil and mint leaves

Thai Lemongrass Soup with Coconut

Shellfish broth:

fish heads*

prawn and lobster shells*

2 carrots

1 parsnip

2 onions

4 stalks parsley

2 ribs celery

1 tsp/5g peppercorns

Thai

Method

1. To make filling, heat peanut oil in a frying pan over a high heat, add shallots, ginger and chili pepper and stir-fry for 2 minutes. Add pork and stir-fry for 4-5 minutes or until pork is brown. Stir in coriander (cilantro) and kechap manis and cook for 2 minutes longer. Remove pan from heat and set aside to cool.

2. To assemble, place 2 tbsp/30g of filling in the center of each wrapper, fold one corner over filling, then tuck in sides, roll up and seal with a few drops of water.

3. Heat vegetable oil in a wok or large saucepan until a cube of bread dropped in browns in 50 seconds. Cook the spring rolls, a few at a time, for 3-4 minutes or until crisp and golden. Drain on absorbent kitchen paper and serve with chili sauce for dipping.

Pork Spring Rolls

Ingredients

24 spring roll (wonton) wrappers, each

5in/12.5cm square vegetable oil for deep-frying

sweet chili sauce (for dipping)

Pork and coriander filling

2 tsp/10ml peanut oil

3 red or golden shallots, chopped

2 tsp/5g finely grated fresh ginger

1 fresh red chili, seeded and chopped

1 lb/500g pork mince

2 tbsp/50g chopped fresh coriander (cilantro) leaves

2 tbsp/50ml kechap manis

Method

1. Dip a rice paper round into cold water, then place on a clean kitchen towel, to absorb any excess moisture.

2. To assemble, place a little of the cucumber, carrot, sprouts, noodles, mint, basil, coriander, and peanuts along the center of each rice paper round leaving a 1in/2cm border. Place a chive (if using) across the center so that the end with the flower hangs over one edge.

3. To roll, fold up one edge of rice paper over filling to form base of roll, then roll up to enclose filling. Repeat with remaining rice paper rounds, filling and chives.

Serve immediately with chili sauce for dipping.

Ingredients

12 large oriental rice paper rounds

Sweet chili sauce (for dipping)

Herbed vegetable filling

2 cucumbers, seeded and cut into
2in/5cm strips

2 carrots, cut into 2in/5cm strips

2oz/60g bean sprouts

2oz/60g rice vermicelli noodles, cooked and drained well

1oz/30g fresh mint leaves

1oz/30g fresh basil leaves

½ oz/15g fresh coriander (cilantro) leaves

4 tbsp/60g chopped roasted peanuts

12 garlic chives with flower (optional)

Herbed Vegetable Rolls

Tip

Traditionally the garlic chive emerges from the open
end of the roll as a garnish. Oriental rice paper is
made from a paste of ground rice and water which is
stamped into rounds and dried. When moistened, the
brittle sheets become flexible.
It is used to make delicacies such as these rolls. Sold
in sealed packets, rice paper can be purchased from
oriental food stores.

Thai

Method

1 Put the vermicelli in a bowl, cover with boiling water, and allow to stand for 10 minutes or until soft. Drain well.

2 Put the ground beef and 3 tbsp of water in a frying pan and cook over a high heat for about 10 minutes or until the beef is tender and cooked. Drain off any excess liquid.

3 Transfer the beef to a bowl, add the beansprouts, lemongrass, lemon juice, fish sauce, green onions (scallions), and water chestnuts.

4 Soak the rice paper wrappers one at a time in a bowl of warm water until soft or allow each guest a bowl of water and let them soak their own.

5 Place a mint leaf at the end of a wrapper, place 2 tbsp/50g of the beef mixture on the wrapper, fold in the ends, and roll up to enclose.

6 Serve with sweet chili sauce.

Lemongrass Beef **Packages**

2 tbsp/50g Chinese (mung bean) vermicelli

350g/12oz lean ground beef

½ cup/4oz/125g beansprouts

2 stalks lemongrass, finely chopped

1 tbsp/15ml lemon juice

1 tbsp/15ml fish sauce

2 green onions (scallions), thinly sliced

1 scant cup/7oz/200g canned water chestnuts, drained and finely chopped

12 rice paper wrappers

12 fresh mint leaves

sweet chili sauce, for dipping

Method

1. Heat a frying pan or chargrill pan over a high heat until hot, add beef, and cook for 1-2 minutes each side, or until cooked to your liking. Set aside to cool.

2. Arrange lettuce, tomatoes, cucumbers, onions, and mint attractively on a serving platter.

3. To make dressing, place lemongrass or lime rind, coriander (cilantro), sugar, lime juice, and soy, chili and fish sauces in a bowl. Mix to combine.

4. Slice beef thinly and arrange on salad, then drizzle with dressing and serve.

Ingredients

1 lb/500g rump or topside steak

6oz/185g mixed lettuce leaves

6oz/185g cherry tomatoes, halved

2 cucumbers, peeled and chopped

2 red onions, sliced

3 tbsp fresh mint leaves

lime and coriander (cilantro) dressing

1 stalk fresh lemongrass, chopped

Thai Beef Salad

or 1 tsp/5g finely grated lemon rind

3 tbsp/45g fresh coriander (cilantro) leaves

1 tbsp/15g brown sugar

2 tbsp/30ml lime juice

3 tbsp/45ml light soy sauce

2 tbsp/30ml sweet chili sauce

2 tsp/5ml Thai fish sauce (nam pla)

Thai

Method

1. Peel the outer layers from the lemongrass stalks and chop the lower white bulbous parts into 3 pieces, discarding the fibrous tops. Shell shrimp, leaving tails attached and reserving the shells for the broth. Cut a slit along the back of each shrimp with a sharp knife and remove the thin black vein. Rinse the shrimp, then refrigerate until needed.

2. Heat the oil in a large saucepan. Fry the shrimp shells for 2-3 minutes, until pink. Add the broth, garlic, ginger, lemongrass, lime rind, green chili pepper, and salt to taste. Bring to boil, then reduce heat, cover, and simmer for 20 minutes.

3. Strain the broth and return to the pan. Stir in the fish sauce and lime juice and bring to the boil. Add the shrimp, reduce the heat, and simmer for 3 minutes or until the shrimp turn pink and are cooked through. Season with pepper and serve garnished with red chili pepper and coriander (cilantro).

Thai Shrimp Soup

Ingredients

2 stalks lemongrass

1½ cups/11oz/300g whole green shrimp , defrosted if frozen

1 tbsp/15ml vegetable oil

4 cups/1¾ pints/1 l chicken broth

1 clove garlic, crushed

1in/2½cm piece fresh root ginger, roughly chopped

2 limes, juice squeezed, rind of 1 grated

1 green chili pepper, deseeded and chopped

salt and black pepper

1 tbsp/15ml Thai fish sauce

1 red chili pepper, deseeded and sliced

2 tbsp/50g chopped fresh coriander (cilantro) to garnish

Method

Heat the olive oil in a large saucepan and add the onion and garlic. Cook for 10 minutes to caramelize gently. Add the chili pepper and coriander stems (finely chopped) and stir until fragrant.

Add the remaining spices and heat until toasted. Add all the pumpkin pieces and stir to coat with spice mixture. Cover with a lid and cook over a low heat for 30 minutes until the pumpkin is beginning to soften and turn brown. Add just enough broth to cover and stir well. Simmer for 1 hour, then add the coconut milk, and simmer for a further 15 minutes. Purée then serve, garnished with extra chili pepper and coriander.

Ingredients

2 tbsp/30ml olive oil

1 large brown onion, chopped

4 cloves garlic, chopped

1 small red chili pepper, finely chopped

4 tbsp/60g coriander

½ tsp/2.5g chili paste

1 tsp/5g ground cumin

Thai-Spiced Pumpkin Soup

1 tsp/5g turmeric

2 cups/1lb/500g pumpkin, diced

2 cups/1lb/500g butternut squash, diced

2 cups/1lb/500g winter squash, diced

6 cups/ chicken broth

1¾ cups/14fl oz/400ml can coconut milk

Thai

31

Method

1. Heat oil in a saucepan over a high heat, add shallots and lemongrass and cook, stirring, for 3 minutes. Stir in galangal or ginger, and broth, then reduce heat and simmer for 5 minutes.

2. Add tofu, mushrooms, beans, beansprouts, and coconut milk and cook over a medium heat for 4 minutes or until beans are tender and soup is heated. To serve, ladle into bowls and scatter with basil and peanuts.

Method

1. Place broth, lemongrass, chili peppers, galangal, or ginger and coriander (cilantro) stalks and leaves in a saucepan and bring to the boil over a medium heat. Add sweet potato and simmer, uncovered, for 15 minutes or until sweet potato is soft.

2. Remove lemongrass, galangal or ginger, and coriander (cilantro) roots, and discard. Cool liquid slightly, then purée soup, in batches, in a food processor or blender. Return soup to a clean saucepan and stir in ½ cup/125 ml/4 fl oz coconut cream and the fish sauce. Cook, stirring, over a medium heat for 4 minutes or until heated. Stir in two-thirds of the reserved coriander leaves.

3. To serve, ladle soup into bowls, top with a little of the remaining coconut cream and scatter with remaining coriander (cilantro) leaves.

Thai Vegetable Soup
Chili Sweet Potato Soup

Ingredients

1 tbsp/15ml chili oil

4 red or golden shallots, chopped

3 stalks fresh lemongrass, cut into pieces, or 1½ tsp/7.5g dried lemongrass, soaked in hot water until soft

4 slices fresh or bottled galangal or fresh ginger

8 cups/3½ pints/2 l vegetable broth

1 cup/8oz/250g firm tofu, cubed

½ cup/4oz/125g oyster mushrooms

4oz/125g snake (yard-long) or green beans, chopped

1oz/30g bean sprouts

1 cup/8fl oz/250ml coconut milk

2 tbsp/30g fresh basil leaves

3 tbsp/45g finely chopped peanuts

Chili Sweet Potato Soup

6 cups/2½ pints/1½ l chicken broth

3 stalks fresh lemongrass, bruised, or 1½ tsp dried lemongrass, soaked in hot water until soft

3 fresh red chilies, halved

10 slices fresh or bottled galangal or fresh ginger

5-6 fresh coriander (cilantro) plants, roots washed, leaves removed and reserved

1 large orange sweet potato, peeled and cut into 2cm/¾in pieces

¾ cup/6fl oz/185ml coconut cream

1 tbsp/15ml Thai fish sauce (nam pla)

Thai

Method:

1 To make dressing, place coriander, sugar, soy, and chili sauces, lime juice, and fish sauce in a bowl and mix to combine. Set aside.

2 Arrange lettuce leaves and cucumber on a serving platter and set aside.

3 Heat oil in a wok over a high heat, add lamb, and stir-fry for 2 minutes or until brown. Place lamb on top of lettuce leaves, drizzle with dressing and serve immediately.

Note:

This salad is also delicious made with pork fillet. Use a vegetable peeler to make long thin slices of cucumber—simply peel off lengthwise strips.

Ingredients

2 cups/8oz/250g assorted lettuce leaves

1 cucumber, sliced lengthwise into thin strips

2 tsp/10ml vegetable oil

1 lb/500g lamb fillets, trimmed of all visible fat, thinly sliced

Warm Thai Lamb Salad

Coriander and chili dressing

2 tbsp/30g chopped fresh coriander

1 tbsp/15g brown sugar

¼ cup/2fl oz /60ml soy sauce

2 tbsp/30ml sweet chili sauce

2 tbsp/30ml lime juice

2 tsp/10ml fish sauce

Thai

Method

1 Peel the mangoes and slice the flesh into thin strips. Run a vegetable peeler down the length of the cucumber to form long ribbons and put in a bowl with the bell pepper, mint, and coriander. Toss, cover, and refrigerate while preparing the rest of the salad.

2 Put the lime juice, ginger, fish sauce, sweet chili sauce, and palm sugar in a jug and whisk to combine.

3 Preheat a broiler, lightly brush the fish fillets with the peanut oil and cook over a high heat for 3-4 minutes on each side or until cooked.
Place some of the salad on each plate and top with fish fillets.

4 Drizzle the dressing over the fish and salad. Serve sprinkled with peanuts.

Thai Fish and Mango Salad

2 small mangoes	2 tbsp/30ml fish sauce
2 small cucumbers	2 tbsp/30ml sweet chili sauce
1 red bell pepper, roasted, peeled and cut into thin strips	1 tbsp/15g grated light palm sugar or brown sugar
2 tbsp/50g fresh mint sprigs	4 fillets (about 9oz/260g each) white fish
2 tbsp/50g fresh coriander sprigs	tbsp/5ml peanut oil
⅓ cup/2½ fl oz/80ml lime juice	2 tbsp/30g unsalted peanuts, roughly chopped
1 tsp/5g fresh ginger, grated	

Thai

Method

1. Cut six 20cm/8in circles from the banana leaves. Make four pinch pleats around the edge of the circle and secure with a toothpick to make a cup. Set aside.

2. Place 1 cup/8fl oz/250ml coconut milk in a saucepan and bring to the boil. Stir in curry paste and mix to combine. Remove from heat, cool slightly, then whisk in eggs. Add fish, lime leaves, sugar, fish sauce and remaining coconut milk and cook, stirring, over a low heat for 5 minutes.

3. Sprinkle the base of banana leaf cups with basil, then divide fish mixture evenly between cups. Place cups in a bamboo steamer and set aside.

4. Half fill a wok with hot water and bring to the boil. Place steamer on a wire rack in wok, cover and steam for 15 minutes. Top each mousse with a little coconut cream, then steam for 5-7 minutes longer or until mousse are firm.

Ingredients

banana leaves, blanched	2 kaffir lime leaves, shredded
2 cups/16fl oz/500ml coconut milk	1 tsp/5g sugar
3 tbsp/45ml Thai red curry paste	2 tbsp/30ml Thai fish sauce (nam pla)
2 eggs, lightly beaten	½ cup/4oz/125g fresh basil leaves
1 lb/500g firm white fish fillets, chopped	½ cup/4fl oz /125ml coconut cream

Steamed Fish Mousse

Tip

If banana leaves are not available

1 cup/8fl oz/250ml capacity ramekins

or custard cups can be used instead.

Thai

Method

1. Place coconut cream, curry paste, lemongrass, and lime leaves in a saucepan and bring to the boil. Reduce heat and simmer for 5 minutes or until fragrant.

2. Add mango and simmer for 3 minutes. Add fish, sugar, and fish sauce and simmer for 3-4 minutes or until fish is cooked. Stir in vinegar and coriander (cilantro) and serve.

Green Mango and Fish **Curry**

Ingredients

1½ cups/12fl oz/375ml coconut cream

1 tsp/5g Thai Green Curry Paste
(see page 78)

1 stalk fresh lemongrass, bruised,
or ½ tsp/2.5g dried lemongrass,
soaked in hot water until soft

4 kaffir lime leaves, finely sliced

1 large green (unripe) mango,
cut into ¼in/5mm thick slices

1 lb/500g firm fish fillets, cut into
2in/5cm cubes

1 tbsp/15g palm or brown sugar

2 tbsp/30ml Thai fish sauce (nam pla)

1 tbsp/15ml coconut vinegar

2oz/60g fresh coriander (cilantro) leaves

Note

Green (unripe) mango and papaya are commonly used in
Thai cooking, as they add a tartness to the finished dish.
If green (unripe) mangoes are unavailable, use tart green
apples or papayas, but on no account use ripe mangoes
as they do not give the same flavor or texture.

Thai

Method

1   Place galangal or ginger, lemongrass, lime leaves, chopped chili peppers, shrimp paste, fish sauce and lime juice in a food processor and process to make a thick paste, adding a little water if necessary.

2   Heat 1 tbsp/15ml oil in a wok or large saucepan over a medium heat, add shallots, garlic, sliced red chili peppers, and spice paste and cook, stirring, for 2-3 minutes or until fragrant. Remove and set aside.

3   Heat remaining oil in wok over a high heat and stir-fry beef, in batches, until brown. Return spice paste to pan, stir in broth and okra, and bring to the boil. Reduce heat and simmer, stirring occasionally, for 15 minutes.

4   Stir in cashews, sugar and soy sauce and simmer for 10 minutes longer or until beef is tender.

Cashew and Chili **Beef Curry**

1¼ in/3cm piece fresh galangal or ginger, chopped or 5 slices bottled galangal, chopped

1 stalk fresh lemongrass, finely sliced, or ½ tsp/2.5g dried lemongrass, soaked in hot water until soft

3 kaffir lime leaves, finely shredded

2 small fresh red chili peppers, seeded and chopped

2 tsp/10g shrimp paste

2 tbsp/30ml Thai fish sauce (nam pla)

1 tbsp/15ml lime juice

2 tbsp/30ml peanut oil

4 red or golden shallots, sliced

2 cloves garlic, minced

3 small fresh red chili peppers, sliced

1 lb/500 g round or blade steak, cut into ¾ in/2 cm cubes

2 cups/16 fl oz/500 ml beef broth

8 oz/250 g okra, trimmed

2 oz/60 g cashews, roughly chopped

1 tbsp/15g palm sugar or brown sugar

2 tbsp/30ml light soy sauce

43

Method

1. Place noodles in a bowl and pour boiling water to cover over them. If using fresh noodles soak for 2 minutes; if using dried noodles soak for 5-6 minutes or until soft. Drain well and set aside.

2. Heat oil in a frying pan or wok over a high heat, add shallots, chili peppers, and ginger and stir-fry for 1 minute. Add chicken and shrimp, and stir-fry for 4 minutes or until cooked.

3. Add noodles, peanuts, sugar, lime juice, and fish and soy sauces and stir-fry for 4 minutes or until heated through. Stir in tofu, beansprouts, coriander (cilantro), and mint and cook for 1-2 minutes or until heated through. Serve with lime wedges.

Ingredients

10oz/315g fresh or dried rice noodles

2 tsp/10ml vegetable oil

4 red or golden shallots, chopped

3 fresh red chili peppers, chopped

2 tbsp/30g shredded fresh ginger

1 cup/8oz/225g boneless chicken breast fillets, chopped

1 cup 8oz/225g raw shrimp, shelled and deveined

2 tbsp/2oz/55g roasted peanuts, chopped

1 tbsp/15g sugar

Pad Thai

4 tbsp/60ml lime juice

3 tbsp/45ml fish sauce

2 tbsp/30ml light soy sauce

½ cup/4oz/125g tofu, chopped

¼ cup/2oz/55g bean sprouts

4 tbsp/60g fresh coriander (cilantro)
leaves

3 tbsp/45g fresh mint leaves

lime wedges to serve

Thai

Method

1. Slice meat from duck, leaving the skin on, and cut into bite-sized pieces. Reserve as many of the cavity juices as possible.

2. Heat oil in a wok over a medium heat, add curry paste, shrimp paste, lemongrass, and chili peppers, and stir-fry for 3 minutes or until fragrant.

3. Add duck and reserved juices and stir-fry for 2 minutes or until coated in spice mixture and heated. Add broccoli or chard, sugar, tamarind, and fish sauce and stir-fry for 3-4 minutes or until broccoli is wilted.

Stir-fried Duck in Greens

Ingredients

2lb/1 kg Chinese barbecued or roasted duck

2 tsp/10ml vegetable oil

1 tbsp/15g Thai Red Curry Paste

1 tsp/15g shrimp paste

1 stalk fresh lemongrass, finely sliced,

or ½ tsp/2.5g dried lemongrass, soaked in hot

water until soft

4 fresh red chili peppers

8oz/250g Chinese broccoli (gai lum) or

Swiss chard, chopped

1 tbsp/15g palm or brown sugar

2 tbsp/30ml tamarind concentrate

1 tbsp Thai fish sauce (nam pla)

Note:

Chinese broccoli (gai lum) is a popular Asian vegetable. It has dark

green leaves on firm stalks often with small white flowers.

The leaves, stalks, and flowers are all used in cooking, however the

stalks are considered to be the choicest part of the plant. To pre-

pare, remove leaves from stalks, and peel, then chop both leaves

and stalks and use as directed in the recipe.

Thai

Method

1 Place chicken in a ceramic or glass dish and set aside.

2 Place chili peppers, garlic, coriander roots, lemongrass, lime juice, and soy sauce in a food processor and process to make paste. Mix paste with coconut cream and pour this over chicken. Marinate for 1 hour.

3 Drain chicken and reserve marinade. Cook chicken over a slow charcoal or gas barbecue or under a preheated broiler on low, brushing frequently with reserved marinade, for 25-30 minutes or until chicken is tender. Serve with chili sauce.

Method

1 Place garlic, coriander, and black peppercorns in a food processor and process to make a paste. Coat chicken with garlic paste and marinate for 1 hour.

2 Heat oil in a wok or frying pan over a high heat until a cube of bread dropped in browns in 60 seconds. Deep-fry the chicken, a few pieces at a time, for 2 minutes or until golden and tender. Drain on absorbent kitchen paper.

3 Deep-fry basil and mint until crisp, then drain and place on a serving plate. Top with chicken and serve with chili sauce.

Chargrilled **Chicken**
Chicken with Garlic and Pepper

Chargrilled chicken

2¼ lb/1 kg chicken pieces

4 fresh red chili peppers, chopped

4 cloves garlic, chopped

2 tbsp/1oz/25g coriander leaves, chopped

2 stalks fresh lemongrass, chopped,
or 1 tsp/5g dried lemongrass soaked
in hot water until soft

3 tbsp/45ml lime juice

2 tbsp/30ml light soy sauce

1 cup/8 fl oz/250 ml coconut cream

1tbsp/15ml sweet chili sauce

Chicken with Garlic and Pepper

4 cloves garlic

3 fresh coriander sprigs

1 tsp/5g crushed black peppercorns

1¼lb/500g chicken breast fillets,
cut into 1¼ in/3 cm cubes

vegetable oil for deep-frying

2 tbsp/1 oz/30 g fresh basil leaves

2 tbsp/1 oz/30 g fresh mint leaves

1tbsp/15ml sweet chili sauce

Cardamon and orange duck

1 Remove meat from duck and cut into bite-sized pieces. Reserve bones, skin, and as much of the juices as possible. Place reserved bones, skin, and juices, stock, chili peppers, galangal or ginger, lemongrass, coriander stems, and roots, cardamom pods, lime leaves, and orange rind in a saucepan and bring to the boil. Reduce heat and simmer, uncovered, for 15 minutes. Strain liquid and set aside. Discard the solids.

2 Heat oil in a wok or large saucepan over a medium heat. Add shrimp and curry pastes and garlic and cook, stirring, for 1-2 minutes or until fragrant.

3 Add duck pieces and stir to coat with spice paste. Add reserved liquid and simmer for 3-4 minutes or until liquid reduces slightly. Stir in orange segments, coriander leaves, and sugar. Serve scattered with green onions (scallions).

Thai green chicken curry

1 Heat oil in a saucepan over a high heat, add onions and cook for 3 minutes or until golden. Stir in curry paste and cook for 2 minutes or until fragrant.

2 Add chicken, basil, lime leaves, coconut milk, and fish sauce, and bring to the boil. Reduce heat and simmer for 12-15 minutes or until chicken is tender and sauce is thick. Serve garnished with extra basil.

3 lb/1½ kg Chinese barbecued or roasted duck

3 cups/1¼ pints/750ml chicken broth

2 small fresh red chili peppers, halved

1¼ in/3 cm piece fresh galangal or ginger, sliced, or 5 slices bottled galangal

2 stalks fresh lemongrass, cut into

1¼ in/3 cm pieces, bruised, or

1 tsp/5g dried lemongrass, soaked in hot water until soft

6 whole coriander plants, washed, stems and roots removed, leaves reserved

6 cardamom pods, crushed

4 kaffir lime leaves, torn into pieces

1 large orange, peeled, all white pith removed from rind, flesh segmented and reserved

1 tbsp/15ml vegetable oil

2 tsp/10g shrimp paste

2 tsp/10g Thai red curry paste

1 clove garlic, minced

1 tsp/5g palm or brown sugar

2 green onions (scallions), cut into thin strips

Cardamom and Orange **Duck**
Thai Green **Chicken Curry**

Thai green chicken curry

1 tbsp/15ml vegetable oil

2 onions, chopped

3 tbsp/45ml Thai green curry paste

2 lb/1 kg boneless chicken thigh

or breast fillets, chopped

4 tbsp/60g fresh basil leaves

6 kaffir lime leaves, shredded

2½ cups/1 pints/600 ml coconut milk

2 tbsp/30ml Thai fish sauce (nam pla)

extra fresh basil leaves

Thai

Chicken Phanaeng Curry

1   Place coconut milk in a saucepan and bring to the boil over a high heat, then boil until oil separates from coconut milk and it reduces and thickens slightly. Stir in curry paste and boil for 2 minutes or until fragrant.

2   Add chicken, beans, peanuts, sugar and fish sauce and simmer for 5-7 minutes or until chicken is tender. Stir in coconut cream, basil and coriander. Serve garnished with slices of chili pepper.

Chicken with Lime and Coconut

1   Place chicken and curry paste in a bowl and toss to coat. Heat oil in a wok or large saucepan over a high heat, add chicken and stir-fry for 4-5 minutes or until lightly browned and fragrant.

2   Add sugar, lime leaves, lime rind, coconut cream and fish sauce and cook, stirring, over a medium heat for 3-4 minutes or until the sugar dissolves and caramelizes.

3   Stir in vinegar and coconut and simmer until chicken is tender. Serve with chili peppers in a dish on the side.

Chicken Phanaeng **Curry**
Chicken with **Lime and Coconut**

Chicken Phanaeng ingredients

2 cups/16 fl oz/500 ml coconut milk
3 tbsp/45ml Thai red curry paste
1 lb/450 g chicken breast fillets, sliced
8 oz/250 g snake (yard-long) or green beans
3 tbsp/45g unsalted peanuts, roasted and finely chopped
2 tsp/10g brown or palm sugar
1 tbsp Thai fish sauce (nam pla)
½ cup/4 fl oz/125 ml coconut cream
2 tbsp fresh basil leaves
2 tbsp fresh coriander leaves
sliced fresh red chili pepper

Chicken with Lime and Coconut ingredients

2¼lb/1 kg chicken thigh or breast fillets, cut into thick strips
1 tbsp/15ml Thai red curry paste
1 tbsp/15ml vegetable oil
3 tbsp/45g palm or brown sugar
4 kaffir lime leaves
2 tsp/10g finely grated lime rind
1 cup/8 fl oz/250 ml coconut cream
1 tbsp/15ml Thai fish sauce (nam pla)
2 tbsp/30ml coconut vinegar
3 tbsp/45g shredded coconut
4 fresh red chili peppers, sliced

Method

1. Grind the cod fillets in a food processor or pound using a pestle and mortar. Add the red curry paste, fish sauce, cornstarch, and egg. Blend again briefly or stir until mixed.

2. Transfer the fish mixture to a bowl and mix together with the shallot and beans. Lightly oil your hands (the mixture is quite sticky), then divide and shape into 8 patties.

3. To make the dipping sauce, mix together the sugar and lime juice, stirring until the sugar dissolves, then stir in the garlic, ginger, peanuts, chili pepper, and soy sauce. Set aside.

4. Heat 1cm/½ in of oil in a large frying pan or wok over a medium to high heat, then fry half of the fish cakes for 3-4 minutes on each side, until golden. Drain on kitchen paper, then cook the remaining cakes. Serve with the dipping sauce.

Thai Fish Cakes
with Peanut Dipping Sauce

Ingredients

12oz/350g skinless cod fillets

1 tbsp/15ml Thai red curry paste

1 tbsp/15ml Thai fish sauce

2 tbsp/10g cornstarch

1 medium egg, beaten

1 shallot, minced

2oz/50g fine green beans, cut into 5mm/¼in lengths

peanut oil for shallow-frying

For the dipping sauce

2 tbsp/10g sugar

juice of 1 lime

1 clove garlic, finely chopped

½in/1cm piece fresh root ginger, finely chopped

1 tbsp/15ml roasted salted peanuts, roughly crushed

1 small red chili pepper, deseeded and finely chopped

2 tbsp/30ml light soy sauce

Thai

Method

1. Heat oil and garlic together in a wok over a medium heat, increase heat to high, add beef and stir-fry for 3 minutes, or until beef turns color.

2. Add beans, lime leaves, sugar, soy, and fish sauces, and stir-fry for 2 minutes or until beans turn color. Stir in coriander (cilantro) and serve immediately.

Ingredients

2 tsp/10ml vegetable oil

2 cloves garlic, crushed

1 lb/500g topside or round steak, cut into thin strips

6oz/185g snake (yard-long) or green beans, cut into 4in/10cm lengths

2 kaffir lime leaves, shredded

2 tsp/10g brown sugar

2 tbsp/10ml light soy sauce

1 tbsp/15ml Thai fish sauce (nam pla)

2 tbsp/30g coriander (cilantro) leaves

Beef and Bean Stir-fry

Tip

Kaffir limes are a popular Thai ingredient. Both the

fruit and the leaves have a distinctive flavor and fra-

grance and are used extensively in cooking.

The leaves are available dried, frozen, or fresh from

oriental grocery stores and some greengrocers.

If kaffir lime leaves are unavailable a little finely grated

lime rind can be used instead.

Thai

Method

1. Peel the outer layer from the lemongrass and chop the lower white bulbous part, discarding the fibrous top. Blend to a paste with the onion, garlic, coriander (cilantro), turmeric, lemon juice, and 1 tsp/5g of salt in a food processor. Alternatively, grind the lemongrass, onion, and garlic with a pestle and mortar, then mix in the other ingredients.

2. Place the chicken in a non-reactive bowl and coat with the paste. Cover and marinate in the fridge for 2 hours, or overnight. If using wooden skewers, soak them in water for 10 minutes.

3. To make the satay sauce, blend the onion and garlic to a paste in a food processor or grind with a pestle and mortar. Heat the oil in a heavy-based saucepan and fry the paste for 5 minutes, stirring. Mix in the chili powder, then the remaining sauce ingredients.
Bring to the boil, stirring, then simmer for 10 minutes.

4. Preheat the broiler to high. Thread the chicken onto 8 skewers. Broil for 10 minutes, turning once, until cooked. Serve with the cucumber and satay sauce.

Chicken **Satays**

Ingredients

1 stalk lemongrass

1 onion, chopped

1 clove garlic, chopped

2 tsp/10g ground coriander (cilantro)

1 tsp/5g turmeric

½ lemon, juice squeezed

salt and black pepper

3 skinless, boneless chicken breasts, cut into

½ in/1cm cubes

½ cucumber, pared into ribbons with a

vegetable peeler, to serve

For the satay sauce

1 small onion, chopped

1 clove garlic, chopped

1 tbsp/15ml peanut oil

1 tsp/5g chili powder

⅔ cup/¼ pint/150ml coconut milk

3oz/75g roasted salted peanuts,
finely ground

1 tbsp/15g soft dark brown sugar

1 tbsp/15ml fresh lemon juice

Method

1. Heat oil in a wok over a medium heat, add curry paste, and stir-fry for
3 minutes or until fragrant.
Add beef to pan and stir-fry for 5 minutes longer or until beef is brown.

2. Stir coconut milk into the mixture and bring to the boil. Reduce heat and
simmer, stirring occasionally, for 15 minutes. Add zucchini (courgettes), red bell
pepper, tomatoes, and green onions (scallions) and cook for 10 minutes longer
or until beef is tender. Stir in basil leaves and serve.

Ingredients

1 tbsp/15ml vegetable oil

1 tbsp/15ml Thai red curry paste

1 lb/500g rump steak, thinly sliced

1½ cups/12fl oz/375ml coconut milk

2 zucchini (courgettes), sliced

1 red bell pepper, chopped

½ cup/4oz/125g cherry tomatoes

4 green onions (scallions), sliced diagonally

12 fresh basil leaves

Coconut **Beef Curry**

Tip

If you do not have time to make your own

curry pastes, use commercially prepared

ones available from supermarkets and

oriental food stores.

Thai

Method

1   Place eggplant in a colander, sprinkle with salt and set aside for 20 minutes. Rinse under cold running water and pat dry on absorbent kitchen paper.

2   Heat oil in a wok or frying pan over a high heat, add onions, chili peppers, garlic and lemongrass and stir-fry for 3 minutes. Add eggplant (aubergines), beans and coconut cream and stir-fry for 5 minutes or until eggplant (aubergines) are tender. Stir in basil.

3 eggplant (aubergines), halved lengthwise

and cut into ½ in/1 cm thick slices

salt

1 tbsp/15ml vegetable oil

2 onions, cut into thin wedges,

layers separated

3 fresh red chili peppers, chopped

Eggplant and Basil **Stir-fry**

2 cloves garlic, sliced

1 stalk fresh lemongrass, chopped,

or ½ tsp dried lemongrass, soaked

in hot water until soft

1 cup/8 oz/250g green beans, trimmed

1 cup/8 fl oz/250ml coconut cream

1½ oz/45g basil leaves

Thai

Method

1. Heat the oil in a nonstick wok or large frying pan. Add the garlic, ginger, and chili pepper and stir-fry for 30 seconds to release the flavors.

2. Add the chicken and Thai seasoning and stir-fry for 4 minutes or until the chicken has colored. Add the bell peppers and zucchini (courgettes) and stir-fry for 1–2 minutes, until slightly softened.

3. Stir in the bamboo shoots and stir-fry for another 2–3 minutes, until the chicken is cooked through and tender. Add the sherry or apple juice, soy sauce, and black pepper, and sizzle for 1–2 minutes. Remove from the heat and stir in the chopped fresh coriander (cilantro), then garnish with more coriander (cilantro).

Thai Spiced Chicken
with Zucchini

Ingredients

1 tbsp/15ml olive oil

1 clove garlic, finely chopped

1in/2½cm fresh root ginger, finely chopped

1 small fresh red chili pepper, deseeded and finely chopped

12oz/350g skinless boneless chicken breasts, cut into strips

1 tbsp/5g Thai 7-spice seasoning

1 red and 1 yellow bell pepper, deseeded and sliced

2 zucchini (courgettes), thinly sliced

7oz/220g can bamboo shoots, drained

2 tbsp30ml dry sherry or apple juice

1 tbsp/15ml light soy sauce

black pepper

2 tbsp/30g chopped fresh coriander (cilantro), plus extra to garnish

Method

1   Place a fish fillet or cutlet in the center of each banana leaf. Top fish with a little each of the garlic, ginger, and lime leaves, then fold over banana leaves to enclose. Place packages over a charcoal barbecue or bake in the oven for 15-20 minutes or until fish flakes when tested with a fork.

2   To make sauce, place mango, shallots, chili peppers, sugar, water, and fish sauce in a saucepan and cook, stirring, over a low heat for 4-5 minutes or until sauce is heated through.

3   To serve, place packages on serving plates, cut open to expose fish and serve with sauce.

Method

1   Make diagonal slashes along both sides of the fish.

2   Place chopped chili peppers, coriander roots, garlic, and black peppercorns in a food processor and process to make a paste. Spread mixture over both sides of fish and marinate for 30 minutes.

3   To make sauce, place sugar, sliced chili peppers, shallots, vinegar, and water in a saucepan and cook, stirring, over a low heat until sugar dissolves. Bring mixture to simmering and simmer, stirring occasionally, for 4 minutes or until sauce thickens.

4   Heat vegetable oil in a wok or deep-frying pan until a cube of bread dropped in browns in 50 seconds. Cook fish, one at a time, for 2 minutes each side or until crisp and flesh flakes when tested with a fork. Drain on absorbent kitchen paper. Serve with chili pepper sauce. Serves 6

4 x 6 oz/185 g firm fish fillets or cutlets

4 pieces banana leaf, blanched

3 cloves garlic, sliced   3 red or golden shallots, chopped

1 tbsp/15g shredded fresh ginger   2 fresh red chili peppers, sliced

2 kaffir lime leaves, shredded   1 tbsp/15g brown sugar

Green mango sauce   ¼ cup/2 fl oz/60ml water

½ small green (unripe) mango, flesh grated   1 tbsp/15ml Thai fish sauce (nam pla)

Fish with Green Mango Sauce
Deep-fried Chili Pepper Fish

Deep-fried chili pepper fish

2 x 1 lb/500g whole fish such as bream, snapper,

whiting, sea perch, cleaned

4 fresh red chili peppers, chopped

4 fresh coriander roots

3 cloves garlic, crushed

vegetable oil for deep-frying

red pepper sauce

⅔ cup/5 ½ oz/170 g sugar

8 fresh red chili peppers, sliced

4 red or golden shallots, sliced

⅓ cup/3 fl oz/90 ml coconut vinegar

⅓ cup/3 fl oz/90 ml water

1 tsp/5g crushed black peppercorns

Thai

Method

1. Heat oil in a wok or frying pan over a medium heat, add garlic and black peppercorns and stir-fry for 1 minute. Add pork and stir-fry for 3 minutes or until brown.

2. Add bok choy, coriander (cilantro), sugar, soy sauce, and lime juice, and stir-fry for 3-4 minutes or until pork and bok choy are tender.

Method

1. Place curry paste in wok and cook, stirring, over a high heat for 2 minutes or until fragrant. Add onions and cook for 2 minutes longer or until onions are soft. Remove from pan and set aside.

2. Heat oil in wok, add pork and stir-fry for 3 minutes or until brown. Remove pork from pan and set aside.

3. Add pumpkin, lime leaves, sugar, coconut milk, and fish sauce to pan, bring to simmering and simmer for 2 minutes. Stir in curry paste mixture and simmer for 5 minutes longer. Return pork to pan and cook for 2 minutes or until heated.

Tip

Bok choy is also known as Chinese cabbage, bock choy, and pak choi. It varies in length from 4–12in/10–30cm. For this recipe, the smaller variety is used. It has a mild, cabbage-like flavor. Ordinary cabbage could be used for this recipe.

Pork in Garlic Pepper
Pork and **Pumpkin Stir-fry**

Ingredients

2 tsp/10ml vegetable oil

4 cloves garlic, sliced

1 tbsp/15g crushed black peppercorns

1 lb/500g lean pork strips

1 lb/500g bok choy (Chinese greens), chopped

4 tbsp fresh coriander (cilantro) leaves

2 tbsp/30g palm or brown sugar

2 tbsp/30ml light soy sauce

2 tbsp/20ml lime juice

Pork and Pumpkin Stir-fry
Ingredients

2 tbsp/30ml Thai red curry paste

2 onions, cut into thin wedges, layers separated

2 tsp/10ml vegetable oil

1 lb/500g lean pork strips

1 lb/500g peeled butternut pumpkin (squash), cut into ¾in/2cm cubes

4 kaffir lime leaves, shredded

1 tbsp/15g palm or brown sugar

2 cups/16fl oz/500ml coconut milk

1 tbsp/15ml Thai fish sauce (nam pla)

Method

1 Cut deep diagonal slits in both sides of the fish. Place lemongrass, ginger, the halved green chili pepper, lime leaves, and coriander plants in cavity of fish.

2 Half fill a wok with hot water and bring to the boil. Place fish on a wire rack and place above water. Cover wok and steam for 10-15 minutes or until flesh flakes when tested with a fork.

3 To make sauce, place red and green chili peppers, garlic, ginger, broth, lime juice, and fish sauce in a small saucepan, bring to simmering over a low heat and simmer for 4 minutes.

To serve, place fish on a serving plate, and spoon the sauce over it.

Ingredients

½ lb/750 g whole fish such as sea perch,

sea bass, tilapia, or red snapper, cleaned

2 stalks fresh lemongrass, chopped,

or 1 tsp dried lemongrass, soaked

in hot water until soft

4 slices fresh ginger

1 fresh green chili pepper, halved

4 kaffir lime leaves, crushed

8 whole fresh coriander plants

Fish with Lime and **Garlic**

Lime and garlic sauce

2 fresh red chili peppers, seeded and chopped

2 green chili peppers, seeded and chopped

3 cloves garlic, chopped

1 tbsp/15g shredded fresh ginger

1 cup/8 fl oz/250 ml fish or

chicken broth

4 tbsp/60ml lime juice

1 tbsp/15ml Thai fish sauce (nam pla)

Thai

1 Place shrimp in a food processor. Using the pulse button, process to roughly chop. Add green onions, ground lemongrass, lime leaves, egg white, fish sauce, lime juice, and chili sauce. Using the pulse button, process until just combined. Transfer mixture to a bowl. Fold in bread crumbs, mint, and coriander.

2 Shape mixture into 1½ in/4 cm diameter patties. Place on a plate lined with plastic wrap or thread 2-3 patties on a lemongrass skewer. Cove and refrigerate for 30 minutes or until patties are firm.

3 Preheat a barbecue to a medium heat. Add patties. Cook for 2-3 minutes each side or until lightly browned. Alternatively, heat a nonstick frying pan over a medium heat. Lightly spray or brush with unsaturated oil and pan-fry, or cook under a medium grill or bake in the oven at 425°F/210°C, but if baking, do not thread onto lemongrass skewers.

4 **Sauce:** Place coriander, green onion, garlic, sugar, vinegar and fish, soy and chili pepper sauces in a bowl. Whisk to combine. Serve with shrimp cakes for dipping.

Thai **shrimp cakes**

2 cups/1¼ lb/500 g raw peeled shrimp, deveined
¼ cup/2oz/50g chopped green onions (scallions)
1 tsp/5g chopped lemongrass
2 kaffir lime or lemon myrtle leaves, soaked in boiling water for 15 minutes, finely chopped,
1 egg white
1 tbsp/15ml fish sauce
1 tbsp/15ml fresh lime juice
1 tsp/5ml sweet chili pepper sauce or to taste
¼ cup/1oz/25g dry bread crumbs, from stale bread
2 tbsp/50g chopped fresh mint
2 tbsp/50g chopped fresh coriander

Coriander Dipping Sauce
2 tbsp/50g chopped fresh coriander
1 green onion, finely chopped
1 clove garlic, crushed
1 tsp/5g brown or palm sugar
¼ cup/60 ml rice or sherry vinegar
2 tsp/10ml reduced-salt soy sauce
½ tsp/2.5ml chili pepper sauce, optional

Method

1. Heat oil in a wok over a medium heat, add onion, lemongrass, and lime leaves, and stir-fry for 3 minutes or until onion is golden.

2. Add curry paste and shrimp paste (if using) and stir-fry for 3 minutes longer or until fragrant. Stir in coconut milk, fish sauce, and sugar. Bring to the boil, then reduce heat, and simmer, stirring frequently, for 10 minutes.

3. Add chicken, bamboo shoots, corn, and basil and cook, stirring frequently, for 15 minutes or until chicken is tender.

Tip

Fresh lemongrass is available from oriental grocery stores and some supermarkets and greengrocers. It is also available dried; if using dried lemongrass soak it in hot water for 20 minutes or until soft before using. Lemongrass is also available in bottles from supermarkets, use this in the same way as you would fresh lemongrass.

Ingredients

1 tbsp/15ml peanut oil

1 onion, minced

1 stalk fresh lemongrass, finely chopped

or 1 tsp/5g dried lemongrass,

soaked in hot water until soft

3 kaffir lime leaves, finely shredded

2 tbsp/30ml Thai Green Curry Paste

(see page 78)

1 tsp/5g shrimp paste (optional)

Green Chicken with Coconut

2 cups/16fl oz/500ml coconut milk

1 tbsp/15ml Thai fish sauce (nam pla)

1 tbsp/15g sugar

1 kg/2lb boneless chicken thigh or breast fillets, cut into 2cm/¾in cubes

1 scant cup/7oz/220g canned bamboo shoots, drained

1¼ cups/10oz/315g canned baby sweet corn, drained

2 tbsp/30g chopped fresh basil

Thai

75

Method

1 Place coriander roots, lemongrass, lime leaves, sugar, water and fish sauce in a saucepan and bring to the boil. Reduce heat and simmer for 10 minutes. Strain, discard solids and set broth aside.

2 Heat oil in a wok or large saucepan over a medium heat, add chili peppers (if using), ginger, and curry paste and stir-fry for 2-3 minutes or until fragrant. Add eggplant (aubergines) and beans and stir to coat with spice mixture. Stir in reserved broth and simmer for 10 minutes or until vegetables are tender. Add tomatoes and tamarind and simmer for 3 minutes or until hot. Add the mint.

6 whole coriander plants, roots removed

and washed, reserve leaves for another use

2 stalks fresh lemongrass, finely sliced, or

1 tsp/5g dried lemongrass, soaked in hot water until soft

6 kaffir lime leaves, shredded

2 tsp/10g palm or brown sugar

3 cups/1¼ pints/750ml water

3 tbsp/45ml Thai fish sauce (nam pla)

2 tsp/10ml peanut oil

Minted **Bean Curry**

3 small fresh green chili peppers, shredded (optional)

2in/5 cm piece fresh ginger, shredded

2 tsp/10ml Thai green curry paste

1 scant cup/7 oz/220g pea eggplant (aubergines)

1 scant cup/7 oz/220g snake (yard-long) or green beans, cut
into 1 in/2.5cm pieces

1¾ cups/14 oz/440g canned tomatoes, drained and chopped

2 tbsp/30ml tamarind concentrate

2oz/60g fresh mint leaves

Thai

Method

1 Place curry paste, shrimp paste, coconut milk, fish sauce, sugar, beef, peanuts, cinnamon, and cardamom into a large saucepan and mix to combine. Bring to simmering over a medium heat, then simmer, stirring occasionally, uncovered, for 40 minutes or until beef is tender.

2 Stir in tamarind mixture and cook for 5 minutes longer.
   Remove cinnamon sticks and cardamom pods before serving.

Ingredients

2 tbsp/30ml Thai curry paste

½ tsp/2.5g shrimp paste

2 cups/16fl oz/500ml coconut milk

1 tbsp/15ml Thai fish sauce (nam pla)

1 tbsp/15g sugar

1 lb/500g rump steak, cut into ¾in/2cm cubes

Thai **Green Curry**

⅔ cup/5oz/155g peanuts, roasted

2 cinnamon sticks

5 cardamom pods

2 tsp/10g tamarind concentrate, dissolved

in 2 tbsp/30ml hot water

Thai

1 Preheat broiler to high.

2 Place mushrooms and wine in a non-reactive saucepan over a medium heat. Bring to the boil. Cook, stirring occasionally, for 2-3 minutes or until mushrooms are tender. Using a slotted spoon, remove mushrooms from wine. Drain well. Set aside. Reserve cooking liquid.

3 Place chili pepper, black pepper, and lime rind in a mortar and grind with the pestle to make a coarse paste. Rub paste over beef. Broil for 1-2 minutes on each side, or until just browned – the beef should be very rare. Remove beef from grill. Rest for 5 minutes. Cut, across the grain, into very thin slices. Set aside.

4 Stir sugar, broth, lime juice, and fish sauce into reserved cooking liquid. Place over a medium heat. Bring to the boil. Remove from heat.

5 Add meat. Turn to coat. Transfer meat mixture to a bowl. Add green onions, basil, mint, and reserved mushrooms. Toss to combine.

6 To serve, pile salad onto a serving platter. Scatter with coriander and peanuts. Accompany with steamed jasmine rice.

Warm Thai Beef and **Mushroom Salad**

2 cups/8oz/250g shiitake mushrooms, trimmed and quartered
2 cups/8oz/250g oyster mushrooms, trimmed and quartered
½ cup/4fl oz/125 ml rice wine (mirin) or dry white wine
1 small fresh red chili pepper, chopped
2 tsp/10g freshly ground black pepper
1 tsp/5g grated lime rind
1¼lb/500g lean beef steak (e.g. fillet, topside or round), trimmed of visible fat
1 tsp/5g sugar

¼ cup/2fl oz/60 ml low-sodium chicken or vegetable broth
1 lime, juice squeezed
2 tbsp/30ml fish sauce
2 green onions or shallots, thinly sliced
1 cup/4oz./20g fresh Thai or sweet basil leaves
2 tbsp/30g fresh mint leaves
2 tbsp/30g chopped fresh coriander
2 tbsp/60g chopped dry roasted unsalted cashews or peanuts

Method:

1   Heat vegetable oil in a wok or large saucepan over a high heat until very hot. Deep-fry noodles, a few at a time, for 1–2 minutes or until lightly golden and puffed. Remove and set aside.

2   Heat sesame oil in a wok or frying pan over a medium heat, add onions and garlic and stir-fry for 4 minutes or until soft and golden. Add pork, chicken and chili pepper flakes and stir-fry for 4 minutes or until pork and chicken are brown and cooked.

3   Add beansprouts, fish sauce, lemon juice, tamarind, and noodles and stir-fry for 2 minutes or until heated through.
    Serve immediately.

Ingredients

vegetable oil for deep-frying

1 cup/8oz/250g rice vermicelli noodles

2 tsp/10ml sesame oil

2 onions, chopped

2 cloves garlic, crushed

6oz/185g lean, boneless pork, chopped

Thai Fried Noodles

6oz/185g boneless chicken breast fillets, chopped

1 tsp/5g dried chili pepper flakes

½ cup4oz/125g bean sprouts

2 tbsp/30ml Thai fish sauce (nam pla)

1 tbsp/15ml lemon juice

2 tsp/10g tamarind concentrate

Thai

Method

1. Combine rice, coriander (cilantro), and black peppercorns to taste, then press into an oiled 7x11in/18x28cm shallow cake pan and refrigerate until set. Cut rice mixture into 1¼x1½in/3x4 cm rectangles.

2 Heat vegetable oil in a large saucepan until a cube of bread dropped in browns in 60 seconds and cook rice cakes, a few at a time, for 3 minutes or until golden.Drain on absorbent kitchen paper.

3 To make topping, place crabmeat, red and green chili peppers, coconut cream, yogurt, lime juice, and fish sauce in a food processor and process until smooth. Stir in lime rind and black peppercorns. Serve with warm rice cakes.

Ingredients

1¾ cups/14oz/440g cooked jasmine rice

1oz/30g fresh coriander (cilantro) leaves, chopped

crushed black peppercorns

vegetable oil for deep-frying

Lime & Crabmeat Topping

6oz/185g canned crabmeat, well-drained

2 fresh red chili peppers, seeded and chopped

Rice Cakes with Lime & Crabmeat

2 small fresh green chili peppers, finely sliced

¼ cup/2fl oz/60 ml coconut cream

2 tbsp/30ml thick plain yogurt

3 tsp/45ml lime juice

3 tsp/14ml Thai fish sauce (nam pla)

3 tsp/15g finely grated lime rind

1 tbsp/15g crushed black peppercorns

Thai

Method

1. Place beef, garlic, ginger, and curry paste in a bowl and mix to combine.

2. Heat sesame and vegetable oils together in a wok over a high heat, add beef mixture and stir-fry for 5 minutes, or until beef is brown. Remove beef mixture from pan and set aside.

3. Add onion to pan and stir-fry over a medium heat for 3 minutes or until golden. Add green bell pepper, red bell pepper, corn, and bamboo shoots and stir-fry for 5 minutes longer, or until vegetables are tender.

4. Return beef to pan, stir in fish sauce, sugar and broth and bring to simmering. Simmer, stirring occasionally, for 10 minutes or until beef is tender.

Tip

When handling fresh chili peppers, do not put your hands near your eyes or allow them to touch your lips. To avoid discomfort and burning, you might like to wear plastic gloves.

Ingredients

750g/1½ lb rump steak, cut into strips

2 cloves garlic, crushed

1 tbsp/5g finely grated fresh ginger

1 tbsp/15ml Thai red curry paste

1 tbsp/15ml sesame oil

1 tbsp/15ml vegetable oil

Thai Chili Pepper Beef

1 onion, cut into wedges

1 green bell pepper, chopped

1 red bell pepper, chopped

1¾ cups/14oz/440g canned baby sweet corn, drained

1 scant cup/7oz/220g canned bamboo shoots, drained

1 tbsp/15ml Thai fish sauce (nam pla)

1 tbsp/15g brown sugar

½ cup/4fl oz/125ml beef stock

Thai

Method

1 Place shallots, chili peppers, galangal or ginger, lime leaves, lemongrass, tamarind, 1 tbsp/15ml lime juice, water, shrimp paste, and dried shrimps in a food processor and process to make a thick paste, adding a little more water if necessary.

2 Place pork in a bowl, add spice paste and toss to coat pork well.

3 Heat oil in a wok or large saucepan over a medium heat, add pork, and stir-fry for 5 minutes or until fragrant and pork is just cooked.

4 Stir in sugar, coconut cream, milk, and fish sauce and simmer, uncovered, for 8-10 minutes or until pork is tender.

5 Add pineapple and remaining lime juice and simmer for 3 minutes or until pineapple is heated. Stir in basil.

Pork and Pineapple with Basil

Ingredients

4 red or golden shallots, chopped

2 fresh red chili peppers, finely chopped

1¼in /3 cm piece fresh galangal or ginger, finely chopped, or 5 slices bottled galangal, chopped

4 kaffir lime leaves

1 stalk fresh lemongrass, tender white part only, finely sliced, or

½ tsp/2.5g dried lemongrass, soaked in hot water until soft

1 tbsp/15g tamarind concentrate

2 tbsp/30ml lime juice

1 tbsp/15ml water

2 tsp shrimp paste

1 tbsp/15g dried shrimp

11oz/350g pork fillets, cut into

1¼in/3cm cubes

1 tbsp vegetable oil

1 tsp palm or brown sugar

1½ cups/12fl oz/375ml coconut cream

½ cup/4fl oz/125ml coconut milk

2 tbsp/30ml Thai fish sauce (nam pla)

½ small (about 1 cup/6½oz/200g) fresh pineapple, cut into ¾in/2cm wide strips

2oz/60g fresh basil leaves

Oven

Over-/ under heat: ca. 220 °C (preheated)

Fan assisted oven: ca. 200 °C (preheated)

Gas oven: stand 4-5 (preheated)

Baking time: 10 minutes

Thai

Method

1 Heat peanut oil and chili pepper oil (if using) in a wok or large saucepan over a medium heat, add tofu and stir-fry until brown on all sides. Remove, drain on absorbent kitchen paper and set aside.

2 Using absorbent kitchen paper, wipe wok or saucepan clean, then add coconut cream and broth and bring to the boil. Stir in curry paste and cook for 3-4 minutes or until fragrant.

3 Add sweet potato, cover, and cook over a medium heat for 8-10 minutes or until sweet potato is almost cooked.

4 Stir in sugar, fish sauce, and lime juice and cook for 4-5 minutes longer or until sweet potato is tender. Stir in basil.

Ingredients

1 tbsp/15ml peanut oil

1 tsp/5ml chili pepper oil (optional)

1¼ cups/10oz/315g firm tofu, cut into ½in/1 cm thick slices

1½ cups/12fl oz/375ml coconut cream

1 cup/8fl oz/250ml vegetable broth

Sweet Potato and Tofu Curry

2 tsp/10g Thai red curry paste

1½ oz/12oz/375g sweet potato, cut into

¾ in/2cm cubes

2 tsp/10g palm or brown sugar

1 tbsp/15ml Thai fish sauce (nam pla)

2 tsp/10ml lime juice

¼ cup/2oz/60g fresh basil leaves

Thai

Method

1. Peel the outer layers from the lemongrass stalks, finely chop the lower white bulbous parts, and discard the fibrous tops. Place the lemongrass, sugar, and ½ cup/4fl oz/125ml of water in a saucepan. Simmer, stirring, for 5 minutes or until the sugar dissolves, then bring to the boil. Remove from the heat and leave to cool for 20 minutes. Refrigerate for 30 minutes.

2. Halve the melon and scrape out the seeds. Cut into wedges, then remove the skin and cut the flesh into small chunks. Slice off the two fat sides of the mango close to the stone. Cut a criss-cross pattern across the flesh (but not the skin) of each piece, then push the skin inside out to expose the cubes of flesh and cut them off.

3. Place the melon, mango and lychees in serving bowls. Strain the lemongrass syrup and pour over the fruit. Decorate with mint.

Oriental Fruit Salad

Ingredients

3 stalks lemongrass

2oz/50g superfine (caster) sugar

1 small cantaloupe melon

1 mango

1¾ cups/14oz/440g can lychees, drained

fresh mint leaves to garnish

Tip

If you're serving a very spicy or rich meal, give your guests this light and unusual fruit salad to finish.

93

Method

1. To make batter, sift flour in a bowl, and make a well in the center. Combine superfine (caster) sugar, milk, and egg, then mix into flour mixture to make a batter of a smooth consistency. Stand for 10 minutes.

2. To make sauce, place sugar and water in a saucepan, and cook over a low heat, stirring constantly, until sugar dissolves. Bring to the boil, then reduce heat and simmer, without stirring, for 5 minutes or until mixture is golden.

3. Remove pan from heat and carefully stir in cream and whisky, if using. Return pan to a low heat and cook, stirring, until combined. Cool.

4. Beat egg white until soft peaks form, then fold into batter. Heat oil in a saucepan until a cube of bread dropped in browns in 50 seconds. Brush bananas with lime juice,dip in batter to coat then drain off excess. Cook bananas in hot oil for 2-3 minutes or until golden. Serve immediately with sauce.

Banana Fritters

Ingredients

4 large firm bananas, cut in half
then split lengthwise

2 tbsp/30ml lime juice

vegetable oil for deep-frying

Batter

1 cup/4oz /125g self-raising flour

2 tbsp/50g superfine (caster) sugar

½ cup/4fl oz/125ml milk

1 egg, lightly beaten

1 egg white

Caramel sauce

½ cup/4oz/125g brown or palm sugar

½ cup/4fl oz/125ml water

½ cup/4fl oz/125ml cream (double)

2 tsp/10ml whisky (optional)

Index